北大版海外汉语教材

初级中文：活学活用
ELEMENTARY CHINESE: LEARNING THROUGH PRACTICE

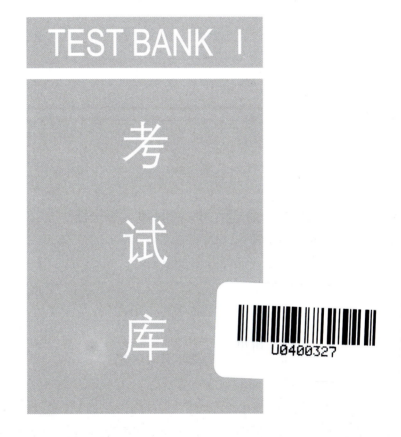

TEST BANK I

考试库

第一册

张湘云　编著
Zhang, Xiangyun

北京大学出版社
PEKING UNIVERSITY PRESS

图书在版编目（CIP）数据

初级中文：活学活用·考试库·第一册/ 张湘云编著. —北京：北京大学出版社，2011.10

（北大版海外汉语教材）

ISBN 978-7-301-18165-2

Ⅰ. 初… Ⅱ. 张… Ⅲ. 汉语—对外汉语教学—习题 Ⅳ. H195.4

中国版本图书馆CIP数据核字（2010）第243070号

书　　　　名：	初级中文：活学活用·考试库·第一册
著作责任者：	张湘云　编著
责 任 编 辑：	邓晓霞 dxxvip@yahoo.com.cn
插 画 绘 制：	张　晗　张婷婷
标 准 书 号：	ISBN 978-7-301-18165-2/H·2709
出 版 发 行：	北京大学出版社
地　　　　址：	北京市海淀区成府路205号　100871
网　　　　址：	http://www.pup.cn
电 子 信 箱：	zpup@pup.pku.edu.cn
电　　　　话：	邮购部 62752015　发行部 62750672　出版部 62754962　编辑部 62767349
印 　刷 　者：	北京宏伟双华印刷有限公司
经 　销 　者：	新华书店
	889毫米×1194毫米　　16开本　　4.75印张　　72千字
	2011年10月第1版　　2011年10月第1次印刷
定　　　　价：	20.00元 (含一张CD-ROM)

未经许可，不得以任何方式复制或抄袭本书之部分或全部内容。

版权所有，侵权必究　　举报电话：010-62752024
　　　　　　　　　　　　电子信箱：fd@pup.pku.edu.cn

ABOUT THE TEST BANK

This Test Bank, a component of *Elementary Chinese: Learning through Practice*, provides instructors a large resource of ideas for information and systematic questions that help to assess students' learning processes and outcomes on the four language proficiencies: listening, speaking, reading and writing.

The Test Bank is written in a flexible manner so that instructors may directly use the questions provided for assessments in their courses, select only certain questions that they find suitable for quizzes or tests, or use the basic format of the questions provided but change vocabulary and expressions. It is entirely the instructor's choice whether or not to use specific items. The Test Bank is an immense resource that the instructor may go to in order to speed the preparation of tests, quizzes, or any other forms of practice with error-free questions and answers. The key for the entire Test Bank is provided to make grading more standardized and efficient.

The entire collection of tests is available as a book and on CD-Rom, the latter to facilitate item selection, modification, and printing.

SPECIAL COPYRIGHT NOTES ON TEST BANK

This Test Bank is one of the components of the series of *Elementary Chinese: Learning through Practice*. All schools and institutions that use this Test Bank to assess teaching and learning of *Elementary Chinese: Learning Through Practice* should require (or provide for) each student to have a copy of this Test Bank. Photocopy of this resource is considered a violation of copyright. The author of the series and Peking University Press would like to make special remarks on this matter.

Zhang, Xiangyun

Emory & Henry College

Peking University Press

关于"考试库"的说明

作为《初级中文：活学活用》这套教材的组成部分，此考试库是为了给使用教材的教师们提供一个能够从中发掘新概念、提取信息及系统化考试题的库源。考试库里的材料便利于考核学生听、说、读、写四种语言技能的学习方法及成果。

考试库的编写方式灵活，教师们可以直接采用库中提供的考题，可以选择部分适当的考题用于考试及小测验，也可以只采用库中提供的基本考试模式，对句子的词汇或短语进行替换。至于是否采用考试库中的某一项题，完全由教师们自行决定。无论教师们做何种选择，考试库是一个供他们使用的丰富材料源地。使用此考试库能帮助教师们加快准备各种考试、测验及其它不同形式练习的速度，并无须为有错题或错答案而顾虑。为使教师们评判考卷的结果更有效、更规范，考试库中为所有的考试题提供了答案。

因为光盘更便利于抽选考试题、进行删改及打印，所以整个考试库有书及光盘两种形式的版本。

"考试库"版权专门说明

本考试库是《初级中文：活学活用》教学系列的组成部分。凡使用本套教材并用本考试库作为检验教学效果的学校及单位应要求(或者为)每一位使用者购买一本考试库。复印使用本考试库属侵犯版权行为，本书作者及北京大学出版社特提醒注意。

张湘云
Emory & Henry College
北京大学出版社

Table of Contents

第一课 ·· 1

第二课 ·· 9

第三课 ·· 17

第四课 ·· 25

第五课 ·· 33

第六课 ·· 41

第七课 ·· 51

第八课 ·· 61

第一课

笔试

第一部分 Part I

姓名 _____ 得分 _____

一、发音。
Pronunciation: Circle the syllable that you hear. 12%

1. mā / má   4. pú / pù   7. wǒ / wò   10. tú / tù
2. tǎ / tà   5. dī / dǐ   8. le / lè   11. lǖ / lǜ
3. ní / nǐ   6. yǔ / yù   9. fú / fù   12. bǔ / bù

二、请写出下列音节。
Write out the syllables that you hear. 10%

1. _____   6. _____
2. _____   7. _____
3. _____   8. _____
4. _____   9. _____
5. _____   10. _____

三、听写。
Dictation: Write out using Chinese the words or sentences that you hear. 15%

1.

2.

6.

7.

3.

4.

5.

8.

9.

10.

四、对不对？

Logical 对 or not logical 不对? Listen carefully and determine if the answer is logical with respect to the question. 12%

1. 对   不对   4. 对   不对
2. 对   不对   5. 对   不对
3. 对   不对   6. 对   不对

五、否定你听到的句子。

Negate the sentences that you hear. 15%

1.

2.

3.

4.

5.

六、把下列各句翻译成中文。
Translate the following sentences into Chinese. 15%

1. I am not a teacher; how about you?

2. Is Li Ming also a teacher?

3. How are you, Wang Xiaowen?

4. My last name is Liu; I am called Liu Wenzhong.

5. Are you not our Chinese teacher?

6. Li Ming is a teacher; are you also a teacher?

7. Hello, Li Ming, (and) Wang Wenzhong!

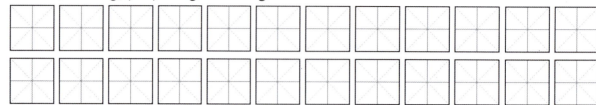

8. Are you students?

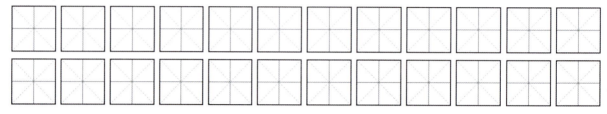

9. You are not students; you are teachers.

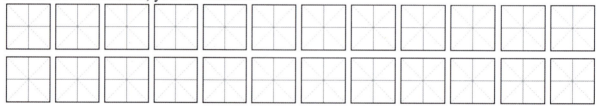

10. Is Li Ming your schoolmate?

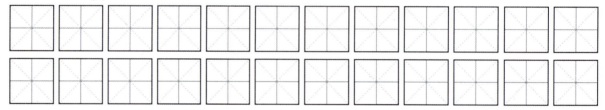

请把第一部分交给老师，然后开始第二部分。
Please turn in this first part before starting the second.

第二部分 Part II

姓名 _____

七、把下列各句翻译成英文。
Translate the following sentences into English. 15%

1. 李明是老师；我也是老师。
   _____

2. 李明，你好吗？
   _____

3. 你不是李明，也不是王小文？
   _____

4. 李明、王小文，你们好！
   _____

5. 你是不是老师？ —— 我不是。我是学生。
   _____

6. 王文明不是老师，是学生。
   _____

7. 你们是小学生吗？ —— 不，我们是中学生。
   _____

8. 你们的中文老师好吗？
   _____

9. 请问，您姓什么？叫什么？
   _____

10. 我是老师，也是学生。

八、文化点滴：请用英文回答下列问题。
Culture Notes: Answer the following questions using English. 6%

1. What is the literary meaning of the Chinese characters '老师?'

2. How is Confucius' birthday celebrated in Hong Kong and Taiwan?

3. What is the meaning of the Chinese saying '一日之师，终身为父?'

口语考试

一、朗读下列句子。
Read aloud the following sentences.

1. 我姓王；我的同学姓李。
2. 你的同学也是我的同学。
3. 刘小明的老师也是你们的老师。
4. 我不是刘学中，我是李学文。
5. 王老师是英文老师，也是中文老师。
6. 同学们，你们好！
7. 请问，您是刘老师吗？
8. 你们是我们的同学。
9. 李老师，您好！
10. 我们学中文，也学英文。

二、用中文回答问题。
Answer the questions using Chinese.

1. 你姓刘吗？
2. 你叫什么名字？
3. 你是学生吗？
4. 你也是老师吗？
5. 刘小明是你的同学吗？
6. 你的英文老师姓什么？
7. 你的中文老师姓什么？
8. 中文好学吗？
9. 英文好学不好学？
10. 你们是王小明的同学吗？
11. 李文中是你们的老师吗？
12. 我是老师，你呢？
13. 我们的老师姓王；你们的老师呢？
14. 请问，你的同学叫什么名字？
15. 我的同学们好，你的同学们好不好？

第二课

笔试

第一部分 Part I

姓名 _____   得分 _____

一、发音。
   Pronunciation: Circle the syllable that you hear. 12%

   1. tāo / táo   4. duǐ / duì   7. kū / kǔ   10. hēi / huī
   2. féi / fěi   5. lóu / lǒu   8. mǎi / mài   11. hē / hé
   3. kāi / gāi   6. lái / lài   9. gǒu / kǒu   12. gē / gè

二、请写出下列音节。
   Write out the syllables that you hear. 10%

   1. _____   6. _____
   2. _____   7. _____
   3. _____   8. _____
   4. _____   9. _____
   5. _____   10. _____

三、听写。
   Dictation: Write out using Chinese the words or sentences that you hear. 15%

   1.

   2.

   6.

   7.

9

3.

4.

5.

8.

9.

10.

四、对不对？

Logical 对 or not logical 不对? Listen carefully and determine if the answer is logical with respect to the question. 12%

1. 对 　　不对　　　　4. 对 　　不对
2. 对 　　不对　　　　5. 对 　　不对
3. 对 　　不对　　　　6. 对 　　不对

五、请用中文回答问题。

Answer the questions using Chinese. 15%

1.

2.

3.

4.

5.

6.

7.

8.

9.

10.

六、把下列各句翻译成中文。
Translate the following sentences into Chinese. 15%

1. Today is my first day in Beijing.

2. My best friend is also her best friend.

3. Do you know my chemistry teacher?

4. They study French literature at Beijing University.

5. Is this the new Chinese grammar book?

6. My English teacher is not American; she is British.

7. Do you know these two characters?

8. What do elementary school students study in their culture class?

9. Let me introduce my students.

10. Today, my teacher is coming to the United States.

请把第一部分交给老师，然后开始第二部分。
Please turn in this first part before starting the second.

第二部分 Part II

姓名 _____

七、把下列各句翻译成英文。
Translate the following sentences into English. 10%

1. 现在我们在学习第二课。
   _____

2. 请你们打开书第九页。
   _____

3. 你介绍一下你的朋友吧。
   _____

4. 我们学习两个新字,好吗?
   _____

5. -你认识高英明吗?   —— 我不认识他。
   _____

6. - 谢谢你!   —— 不谢。
   _____

7. 你们学习汉语,也学习中国文化吗?
   _____

8. 谁不认识张大卫?
   _____

9. 我们学习第一课的语法。
   _____

10. 他们是我的新同学。

　　_____

八、文化点滴：请用英文回答下列问题。
　　Culture Notes: Answer the following questions using English. 10%

1. How do Chinese parents name their children?

　　_____

2. What do the following two names tell you: 王京生 and 黄学明?

　　_____

3. What can one understand from these three names: 张英明, 张文明 and 张新明?

　　_____

口语考试

一、朗读下列句子。
Read aloud the following sentences.

1. 张大卫是美国人，现在他在中国人文大学学习中文。
2. 她姓谢，叫谢文美。她是我的大学同学。
3. 请你介绍一下你的朋友。
4. 这是我们英文语法课的老师，他姓高。
5. 他们在上英文课，我们在上法语课。
6. 同学们，请你们打开书，第六页。
7. 他是我们的汉语课老师，不是我们的化学课老师。
8. 中国人学习汉语，英国人、美国人、法国人也学习汉语。
9. 谢谢你的介绍。
10. 张朋是大学老师，不是中学老师。

二、用中文回答问题。
Answer the questions using Chinese.

1. 你是北京大学的学生吗？
2. 现在谁在上课？
3. 你学习中文，你的朋友也学习中文吗？
4. 你认识我的朋友吗？
5. 谁是你的好朋友？
6. 你是中国人吗？
7. 高小英是美国人吗？
8. 你的汉语书是新书吗？
9. 这是谁的语法书？
10. 那是老师的书吗？
11. 你朋友是中学老师吗？
12. 刘文英是谁的名字？
13. 汉语的语法好学吗？
14. 谢大朋是我的同学，谁是你的同学？
15. 我们认识王老师，你们呢，也认识王老师吗？

第三课

第一部分 Part I

姓名 _____   得分 _____

一、发音。

Pronunciation: Circle the syllable that you hear. 9%

1. qiū / qiú   4. liǎo / lǎo   7. jiǎ / jiǎo
2. xiá / xià   5. biē / bēi   8. qué / què
3. jiā / jiǎ   6. xuē / xué   9. nǎo / niǎo

二、请写出下列音节。

Write out the syllables that you hear. 10%

1. _____   6. _____
2. _____   7. _____
3. _____   8. _____
4. _____   9. _____
5. _____   10. _____

三、听写。

Dictation: Write out using Chinese the words or sentences that you hear. 10%

1.   6.

2.   7.

3.

4.

5.

8.

9.

10.

四、对不对？

Logical 对 or not logical 不对? Listen carefully and determine if the answer is logical with respect to the question. 12%

1. 对 不对 4. 对 不对
2. 对 不对 5. 对 不对
3. 对 不对 6. 对 不对

五、请用中文回答问题。

Answer the questions using Chinese. 15%

1.

2.

3.

4.

5.

6.

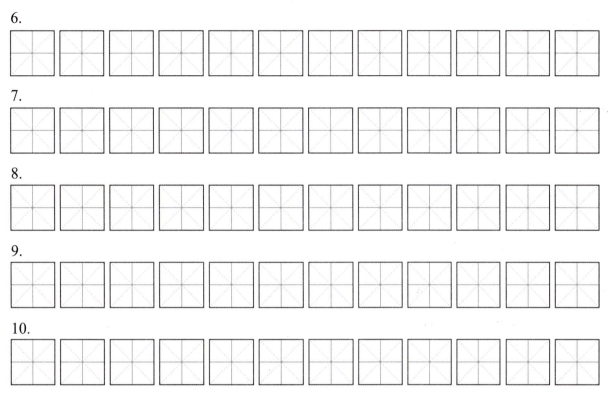

7.

8.

9.

10.

六、把下列各句翻译成中文。
Translate the following sentences into Chinese. 15%

1. My (elder) sister is 24 years old, and she is an elementary school teacher.

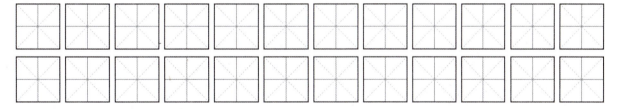

2. This lawyer works together with my father.

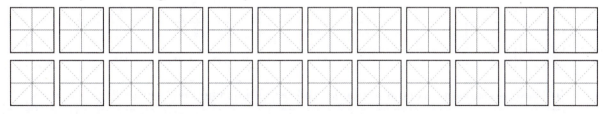

3. Is this your family picture?

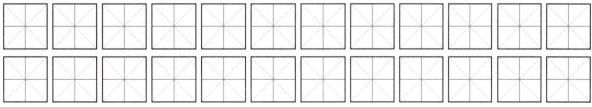

4. Is this your grammar book or the teacher's?

5. His (younger) sister does not work at a bank; she works at a law firm.

6. Is your (elder) brother the oldest child in your family?

7. Do you know her (paternal) grandparents?

8. How old are your parents?

9. These two doctors work at the same（同一个）hospital.

10. Where does your family live?

七、请用中文介绍一下你的家人。
Introduce your family using Chinese. 9%

我的家人

请把第一部分交给老师，然后开始第二部分。
Please turn in this first part before starting the second.

第二部分　Part II

姓名 _____

八、请用适当的量词填空（每个量词只能用一次）。
Fill in the blanks with appropriate measure words (each word can be used only once). 10%

1. 那是 一 _____ 银行。

2. 老师有五 _____ 学生。

3. 这是 一 _____ 大学。

4. 他给我们三 _____ 照片。

5. 我家有六 _____ 人。

九、文化点滴：请用英文回答下列问题。
Culture Notes: Answer the following questions using English. 10%

1. Approximately how many Chinese surnames are currently in use in the world?
   _____

2. What are the two different kinds of Chinese surnames?
   _____

3. Name two to three popular Chinese surnames.
   _____

4. Identify the first and last name in the name 'Deng Xiaoping.'
   _____

5. Why do some Chinese names have two surnames?
   _____

口语考试

一、朗读下列句子。
   Read aloud the following sentences.

   1. 这是一家医院，不是一所大学。
   2. 李银生有两个姐姐，一个弟弟；他没有哥哥，也没有妹妹。
   3. 我家只有三口人：我爸爸、妈妈和我。
   4. 这张照片是刘文明家的全家福。
   5. 这三个人中，谁是律师？谁是医生？谁是老师？
   6. 今天是王安娜的生日，不是高大年的生日。
   7. 你朋友姓张，还是姓王？
   8. 这是北京第二医院，不是北京第六医院。
   9. 这所医院有三十四个医生。
   10. 他们有两个女孩子，没有男孩子。

二、用中文回答问题。
   Answer the questions using Chinese.

   1. 你家有几口人？
   2. 你爸爸妈妈做什么工作？
   3. 你爷爷奶奶是医生吗？
   4. 你认识我的律师吗？
   5. "全家福"是什么？
   6. 你和谁一起学习中文？在哪儿学习中文？
   7. 你的哥哥姐姐是大学生吗？
   8. 医生在医院工作，律师在哪儿工作？
   9. 这是谁的照片？
   10. 你没有朋友吗？
   11. 谁在银行工作？
   12. 你爸爸妈妈多大岁数？
   13. 高新明是你的哥哥还是你的弟弟？
   14. 你爸爸妈妈有几个孩子？几个男孩子？几个女孩子？
   15. 你认识一个好律师吗？

第四课

笔试

第一部分 Part I

姓名 _____   得分 _____

一、发音。
Pronunciation: Circle the syllable that you hear. 9%

1. zāi / cāi   4. jìn / jùn   7. sǒu / zǒu
2. cū / zū   5. bān / pān   8. mén / mèn
3. tán / tǎn   6. qīn / qín   9. sūn / zūn

二、对不对?
Logical 对 or not logical 不对? Listen carefully and determine if the answer is logical with respect to the question. 12%

1. 对   不对   4. 对   不对
2. 对   不对   5. 对   不对
3. 对   不对   6. 对   不对

三、听力。
Choose "yes" or "no" after listening to the passage and comments. 9%

1. 对   不对   2. 对   不对   3. 对   不对

四、把下列各句翻译成中文。
Translate the following sentences into Chinese. 15%

1. I wish you Happy Birthday!

25

2. How about we go together to Chang Cheng Park tomorrow?

3. Do you know how to make a cake?

4. I heard that this is the best Italian restaurant in Beijing.

5. What did you say to them?

6. Do you know what she likes the best?

7. At his home, no one likes to cook.

8. This student works in a Japanese restaurant.

9. What's the date and day for today?

10. We plan to go to the Great Wall next Saturday.

五、请用中文写一篇短文 (至少十五个句子)，介绍一个家人的生日。
   Write a mini-composition (with at least 15 sentences) using Chinese about a family member's birthday. 15%

我 _____ 的生日

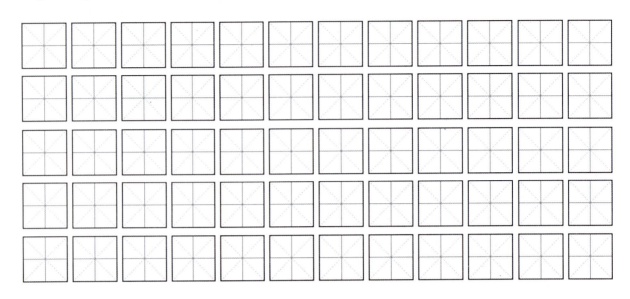

请把第一部分交给老师，然后开始第二部分。
Please turn in this first part before starting the second.

第二部分 Part II

姓名 _____

六、请用适当的词填空。
Fill in the blanks with appropriate words. 10%

1. 你的生日是 _____？

2. 这是 _____ 照片。

3. 谢谢你！ —— 不_____。

4. 这瓶花很 _____。

5. 你喜欢做 _____ 饭？

6. 你找 _____？

7. 你去 _____ 上海吗？

8. 哪家法国餐馆好？请你给我们 _____ 一个。

9. _____ 是中国最长的河 (hé: river)。

10. 他们 _____ 学习汉语？

七、在：这个字在每个句子里是动词还是介词？
Is the character "在" a verb or preposition in each sentence? 10%

1. 他在中国。　　　　　　　　　verb　　preposition

2. 他在美国学习英语。　　　　　verb　　preposition

3. 谁在家？　　　　　　　　　　verb　　preposition

4. 生日卡在哪儿？　　　　　　　verb　　preposition

5. 我弟弟在北京住。　　　　　　verb　　preposition

八、就划线部分提问题。
Ask a question about each underlined part. 10%

1. <u>江小明</u>是我的好朋友。

2. 我们给姥姥买了一瓶花。

3. 这个学期有十六个星期。

4. 周大利家在上海住。

5. 大卫想去中国学习中医。

6. 这是一张全家福。

7. 他们打算和我们一起去长城。

8. 我是我们家的老二。

9. 爸爸最喜欢做饭。

10. 我知道他是一个好学生。

九、文化点滴：请用英文回答下列问题。

Culture Notes: Answer the following questions using English. 10%

1. Why is it believed that the abacus was invented by the Chinese?

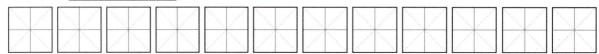

2. What is the difference between the lower beads and upper ones on a Chinese abacus?

   _____

3. What kind of arithmetic functions can be performed on a Chinese abacus?

   _____

4. How is the abacus viewed in Chinese culture?

   _____

5. Which one of the following words is abacus?

   _____

   (a) 算术   (b) 算盘   (c) 打算   (d) 数学

口语考试

一、朗读下列句子。
   Read aloud the following sentences.

   1. 赵长江打算星期六请他的女朋友去一家意大利餐馆吃饭。
   2. 我的朋友们祝我生日快乐,我说:"谢谢你们!"
   3. 我有英国朋友、日本朋友、法国朋友,也有意大利朋友。
   4. 这是我姐姐二十岁生日那天照的照片。
   5. 周老师的中文课上有十八个学生。
   6. 你买的花漂亮,蛋糕漂亮,生日卡也很漂亮。
   7. 你看,这个花瓶里没有花。
   8. 爷爷生日那天吃了长寿面。
   9. 我不认识他们,可是我知道谁是哥哥,谁是弟弟。
   10. 再见,王大利! 明天见!

二、用中文回答问题。
   Answer the questions using Chinese.

   1. 今天是九月二十号,明天呢?
   2. 那个公园的名字是什么?
   3. 孩子们喜欢吃蛋糕吗?
   4. 几月几号是你的生日?
   5. 你喜欢吃中国饭、法国饭、美国饭、日本饭还是意大利饭?
   6. 我和同学们打算下个星期去长城,你想和我们一起去吗?
   7. 你觉得面条好吃吗?
   8. 一个星期有七天,两个星期呢?
   9. 明天是你妈妈的生日,你打算给她买什么?
   10. 你知道李明的生日是几月几号吗?
   11. 中国人过生日吃长寿面,意大利人也吃长寿面吗?
   12. 赵长江和赵长城,谁是哥哥? 谁是弟弟? 你知道吗?
   13. 你想买几张新年卡?
   14. 我觉得这个蛋糕很好吃,你想吃吗?
   15. 我觉得这个老师说汉语很快,你觉得呢?

第五课

笔试

第一部分　Part I

姓名 _____　　　　得分 _____

一、发音。
Pronunciation: Circle the syllable that you hear. 9%

1. chūn / chū
2. rú / rù
3. shǎng / shěng
4. zhài / zài
5. zhēn / zhēng
6. róng / yǒng
7. rāng / rēng
8. chāng / zhāng
9. shì / zhì

二、对不对？
Logical 对 or not logical 不对? Listen carefully and determine if the answer is logical with respect to the question. 12%

1. 对　　不对
2. 对　　不对
3. 对　　不对
4. 对　　不对
5. 对　　不对
6. 对　　不对

三、听力。
Choose "yes" or "no" after listening to the passage and comments. 9%

1. 对　　不对　　　2. 对　　不对　　　3. 对　　不对

四、把下列各句翻译成中文。
Translate the following sentences into Chinese. 15%

1. Students have to come to <u>school</u> (学校) everyday.

33

2. I love to solve math problems.

3. American geography is my favorite course.

4. It's twenty to seven o'clock now.

5. He is taking five courses this semester, so he is busy.

6. How about we have lunch together?

7. What's the most difficult course for you?

8. I plan to take a political science course next semester.

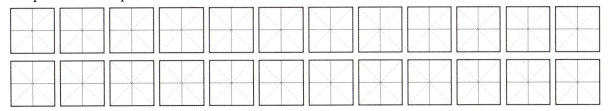

9. She likes none of those three classes.

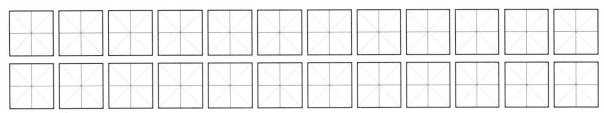

10. I have two classmates who have the last name "何."

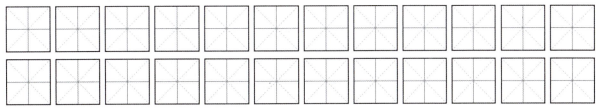

五、请用中文写一篇短文 (至少十五个句子)，介绍你这个学期上的课。
Write a mini-composition (with at least 15 sentences) using Chinese about the courses you are taking this semester. 15%

我这个学期的课

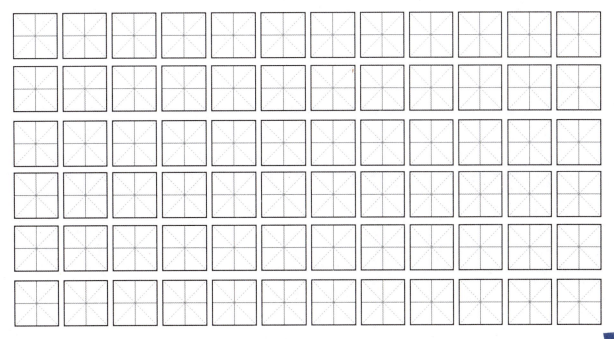

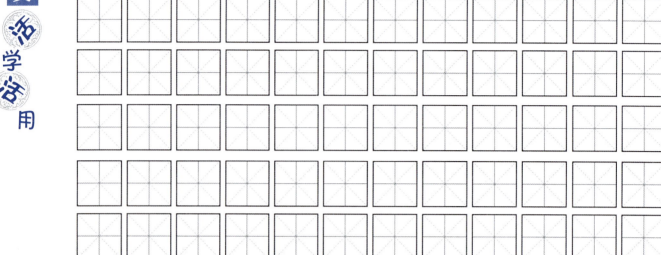

请把第一部分交给老师，然后开始第二部分。
Please turn in this first part before starting the second.

第二部分 Part II

姓名 _____

六、请用适当的词填空。
Fill in the blanks with appropriate words. 15%

1. 现在是 _____ 一刻六点钟。

2. 我很忙，_____ 我还是想来给你过生日。

3. _____ 他体育不好，所以他不喜欢体育课。

4. 现在四点 _____ 五分。

5. 今天我们有四 _____ 课。

6. 你觉得 _____ 门课最有意思？

7. 你们家每天 _____ 吃中国饭吗？

8. 现在不是八点二十，是八点 _____ 。

9. 回头 _____ ！

10. 今天 _____ 三十号了。

七、就划线部分提问题。
Ask a question about each underlined part. 10%

1. <u>物理</u>课不难。

2. 我们<u>八点钟</u>上第一节课。

3. 新年是<u>一个</u>节日。

4. 法国文学<u>史</u>很有意思。

5. "中医"的意思是"中国医学"。

6. 钟济生是我们的物理老师。

7. 化学课和生物课一样难。

8. 我每天五点钟回家。

9. 他喜欢在家里看书。

10. 妹妹给我开门。

八、文化点滴：请用英文回答下列问题。
Culture Notes: Answer the following questions using English. 15%

1. How many ethnic groups are there in China?

2. What is the concept of 'minorities' in Chinese culture?

3. What is the name of the ethnic group that conquered China during the Qing Dynasty (1644-1911)?

4. What is the name of the ethnic group that lives especially in Ningxia?

5. Which ethnic group lives in Xinjiang?

口语考试

一、朗读下列句子。
   Read aloud the following sentences.

   1. 今天上午我很忙，有生物、地理和历史三门课。
   2. "政治经济"是一门课，不是两门课。
   3. 现在差两分钟九点，我得去上美术课了。
   4. 我们差不多天天都是差一刻钟一点吃中午饭。
   5. 现在我们这里是上午八点，北京是晚上八点。
   6. 何小莉是我音乐课上的同学；她不只是音乐好，体育也很好。
   7. 我每个学期都上一门历史课。我学了英国、美国和法国历史；下个学期打算学习中国历史。
   8. 有人问我物理和数学哪门课难。我说："差不多，这两门课都不容易。"
   9. 这个学期我上五门课。星期一、三、五我有三节课；星期二和四只有两节课。
   10. 周觉文有很多政治、历史和地理知识，所以他在经济课上也是一个好学生。

二、用中文回答问题。
   Answer the questions using Chinese.

   1. 你觉得数学课有意思，还是物理课有意思？
   2. 你们几点钟有体育课？
   3. 谁是你们生物课的老师？
   4. 我知道你妈妈是音乐老师，你爸爸呢？他也是老师吗？
   5. 这个学期你上几门课？今天你有几节课？
   6. 在你的六门课里，哪门课最难？哪门课最容易？哪门课最有意思？
   7. 在地理课上，你们在学习哪国地理？
   8. 这个学期你有几个男老师？几个女老师？
   9. 你几点钟吃中午饭？你几点钟吃晚饭？
   10. 你喜欢音乐和体育吗？
   11. 十二点钟你有课吗？我们一起吃中午饭，好不好？
   12. 我听说你的数学很好，你想不想上物理课？
   13. 我是一个新学生，你能不能给我介绍一下什么课有意思，什么课没有意思？
   14. 我知道你上了英国和美国文学课，我也知道你在学习法语；你想不想上一门法国文学课？
   15. 这是一道很难的数学题。你想试试解这道题吗？

第六课

笔试

第一部分 Part I

姓名 _____   得分 _____

一、发音。

Pronunciation: Circle the syllable that you hear. 9%

1. kuāng / kāng   4. huá / huái   7. kòu / kuò
2. qǐng / qiáng   5. diǎn / diàn   8. bēng / bīng
3. zhōng / zhēng   6. guàn / gàn   9. shuāi / shuān

二、对不对？

Logical 对 or not logical 不对? Listen carefully and determine if the answer is logical with respect to the question. 12%

1. 对   不对   4. 对   不对
2. 对   不对   5. 对   不对
3. 对   不对   6. 对   不对

三、听力。

Choose "yes" or "no" after listening to the passage and comments. 9%

1. 对   不对   2. 对   不对   3. 对   不对

四、请用中文回答问题。

Answer the questions using Chinese. 20%

1.

2.

3.

4.

5.

6.

7.

8.

9.

10.

五、把下列各句翻译成中文。

Translate the following sentences into Chinese. 15%

1. Those two exercises are the same.

2. He told me that he likes to learn foreign languages.

3. Chinese pronunciation is hard to learn because of the four tones.

4. Sometimes I think the teacher's requirement is too high (太高了).

5. Our school starts on August 23 this year.

6. In addition to the new words, we have studied grammar today.

7. We are in the elementary math class.

8. I have just gotten to know Wendy.

9. How much time do you spend each day on your homework?

10. The two verbs are completely different.

六、请用中文写一篇短文 (至少一百个字)，介绍你们在中文课上做什么。
Write a mini-composition (with at least 100 characters) using Chinese about what you do in your Chinese class. 15%

在中文课上

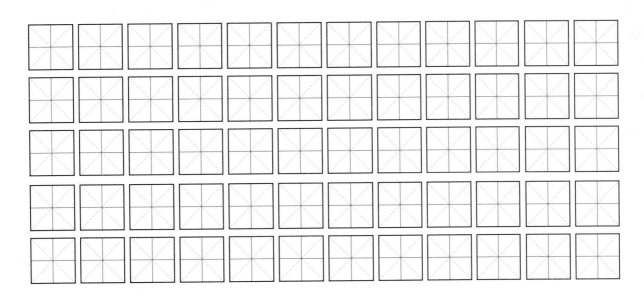

请把第一部分交给老师，然后开始第二部分。
Please turn in this first part before starting the second.

第二部分 Part II

姓名 _____

七、就划线部分提问题。
Ask a question about each underlined part. 10%

1. 我爸爸在<u>大学</u>教物理。

2. 这个课文<u>很长</u>。

3. <u>这个</u>活动很有意思。

4. 我们八点钟开始<u>上课</u>。

5. 老师要求学生们<u>尽量多说中文</u>。

6. <u>我爸爸</u>的工作是 (写作 creative writing)。

7. 我有<u>中文</u>作业。

8. 现在我们练习<u>发音</u>。

9. "花"字是一个姓。

10. 我不喜欢这个考试。

八、文化点滴：请用英文回答下列问题。

Culture Notes: Answer the following questions using English. 10%

1. What is the pronunciation and meaning of this character: '福'?

   _____

2. At what occasion is the '福' character most seen?

   _____

3. Why was the page not punished when he posted the '福' character upside-down?

   _____

口语考试

一、朗读下列句子。
   Read aloud the following sentences.

   1. 在英语语法和初级数学课上我们常常有小测验。
   2. 今年是我们第二年学习汉语，也就是说我们在上中级班的汉语课。
   3. "买"和"卖"两个字的发音截然不同，我得多练习。
   4. 在中文课上，有一个活动我和我的同学们都喜欢；这个活动就是学唱中国歌。
   5. 汉语老师要求学生们听、说、读、写都会，这个要求很高。
   6. 我每天花四十分钟到一个小时做物理课的作业；我的同学们差不多也花这么多时间。
   7. 在历史课上，我们每学完一课就考一次试。这个学期我们学了六课，所以考了六次试。
   8. 打算的"打"字是第三声；大学生的"大"字是第四声。现在请你们说：大学生们打算学习写大字。
   9. 一年级有二十八个学生学习汉语；二年级有十九个。我不知道三年级有多少个学生学习汉语。
   10. 教我们音乐课的老师是一个意大利人。有时候他教我们唱意大利歌。

二、用中文回答问题。
   Answer the questions using Chinese.

   1. 今天在中文课上，除了学习发音以外，你们还干什么了？
   2. 你喜欢和谁一起用汉语做对话？
   3. 做作业的时候你喜欢听音乐吗？
   4. 请你说说考试和测验有什么一样，有什么不一样，好吗？
   5. 哪个老师给你们留作业多？哪个老师给你们留作业少？
   6. 在你们的汉语班里，谁的汉字书写最漂亮？
   7. 你几岁开始学习外语的？你学的第一门外语是什么？
   8. 老师要求我们每天学习二十个汉字。你觉得这个要求高吗？
   9. 你的名字是谁起的？

10. 考试的时候，你的同学问你："留"字怎么写。你能告诉他/她吗？
11. 中文的发音和英文的发音一样吗？有什么一样？有什么不一样？
12. 在中文课上你们常常做什么？有什么活动你喜欢？有什么活动你和你的同学们都不喜欢？
13. 除了中文以外，你还会说什么外语？你在哪里学的这门语言？什么时候学的？
14. 我听说你在学习汉语，你能不能给我介绍一下你怎么学习这门语言？
15. 你打算去中国学习汉语吗？你觉得去中国学汉语和在这里学习汉语会有什么不一样？

第七课

第一部分　Part I

姓名 _____　　　得分 _____

一、发音。
Pronunciation: Circle the syllable that you hear. 5%

1. wǒ pǎo / wō pào
2. ní tiāo / nǐ tiào
3. tà lài / tā lái
4. bǎ dǎo / bào dào
5. běi hǎi / bèi hài

6. tián àn mèn / tiān ān mén
7. huǒu chē / huò chē
8. fēi jī / fěi jí
9. rèn xīng dǎo / rén xíng dào
10. diàn yǐng yuàn / diān yíng yuān

二、对不对？
Logical 对 or not logical 不对? Listen carefully and determine if the answer is logical with respect to the question. 12%

1. 对　　　不对
2. 对　　　不对
3. 对　　　不对

4. 对　　　不对
5. 对　　　不对
6. 对　　　不对

三、听力。
Choose "yes" or "no" after listening to the passage and comments. 9%

1. 对　　不对　　　2. 对　　不对　　　3. 对　　不对

51

四、把下列各句翻译成中文。

Translate the following sentences into Chinese. 15%

1. Every day we come to school on time.

2. You cannot make phone calls in the library.

3. The basketball game will start very soon.

4. Every time he goes out, he does not forget to bring his cell phone with him.

5. Too bad, I forgot to buy the cake.

6. In addition to the new words, we have studied grammar today.

7. This is our own business (affair), we must take care of (办) it ourselves.

8. This number is too long; it's not easy to remember it.

9. Whom are you waiting for here?

10. Play ping-pong is my favorite activity.

五、请用中文写一篇短文(至少一百个字)，说说你和你的同学们下课以后喜欢做什么。
Write a mini-composition (with at least 100 characters) using Chinese about what you and your schoolmates like to do after classes. 15%

下课以后

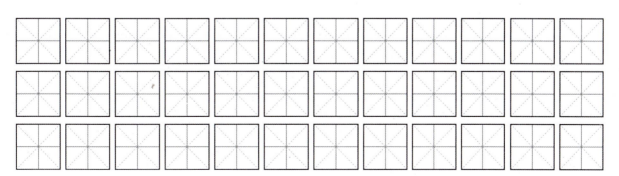

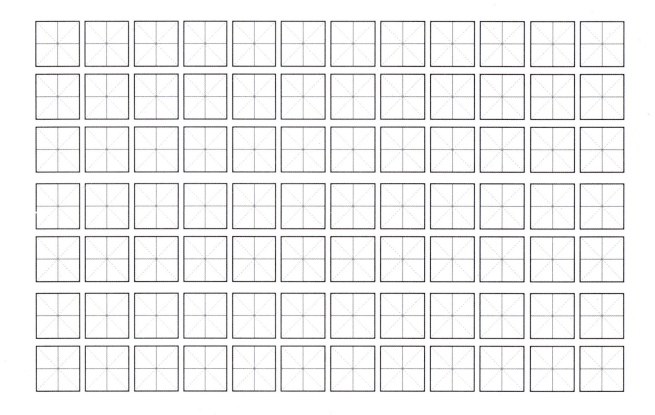

请把第一部分交给老师，然后开始第二部分。
Please turn in this first part before starting the second.

第二部分　Part II

姓名 _____

六、请用适当的量词填空。
Fill in the blanks with appropriate measure words. 10%

1. 这 _____ 学校有八百多个学生。

2. 你们家有几 _____ 人？

3. 昨天我买了两 _____ 书。

4. 大家都喜欢这 _____ 贺年卡。

5. 我们一 _____ 星期打一 _____ 篮球。

6. 这个学期我有五 _____ 课。不过今天我只有三 _____ 课。

7. 我们喜欢这 _____ 餐馆。

8. 那 _____ 花很漂亮。

9. 今天你们学了多少 _____ 生词？

10. 这个老师会四 _____ 外语。

七、请用适当的量词填空。
Fill in the blanks with appropriate words. 15%

1. 上课的时候，你们用中文 _____ 用英文回答老师的问题？

2. _____ 我没有复习，_____ 考试没考好。

3. _____ 汉语以外，你还学习什么外语？

4. 我很喜欢这门课，_____ 这个学期我没有时间上 (这门课)。

5. 请你们做练习三和四。_____ 还有课文后面的问题。

6. 你能不能快一点？_____ 我们就不能按时到了。

7. 这本书不容易读，_____ 很有意思。你会喜欢的。

8. 这个学期你上六门课？对，_____ 我很忙。

9. 明天我不能来上课，_____ 我有一个数学比赛。

10. 今天我们有英文、中文、历史 _____ 音乐课。

八、就划线部分提问题。
Ask a question about each underlined part. 10%

1. <u>下课以后</u>学生们玩球。

2. 他在办公室门口等<u>老师</u>。

3. 今天妈妈忘了带<u>手机</u>。

4. 我和师小莉约好<u>九点钟</u>见面。

5. 朋友们的电话号码都在<u>我的手机里</u>。

6. 我得买这本书，<u>因为图书馆里没有</u>。

7. 他找老师<u>问问题</u>。

8. <u>电话铃</u>响了。

9. 我怕<u>他们不能按时来</u>。

10. 我记住了<u>马可明</u>的生日。

九、文化点滴：请用英文回答下列问题。

Culture Notes: Answer the following questions using English. 10%

1. Why was the Great Wall built?

   _____

2. What did people do to the Great Wall during Ming Dynasty?

   _____

3. What is the length of the Great Wall?

   _____

4. What do you know about Meng Jiangnu (孟姜女)?

   _____

5. Name two to three provinces that the Great Wall runs through.

   _____

口语考试

一、朗读下列句子。
　　Read aloud the following sentences.

1. 我们班有一个同学来上课的时候常常忘带书；大家都叫他/她"马大哈"。
2. 我和同学们都喜欢打乒乓球，可是打得最好的是钟大友。
3. 乒乓球和篮球都是体育活动，可是玩的方法截然不同。
4. 我记住了马明初的电话号码。他的号码是：6428-0127。
5. 什么，现在都四点十分了？糟糕，我忘了去老师的办公室。
6. 我知道在我回答老师的问题之前你就想好了怎么回答老师。
7. 老师等了半天，还是没有人回答他的问题。
8. 老师留完作业之后问我们："大家能按时交作业吗。"除了史复生之外，同学们都回答说："能。"
9. 两分钟以后，老师还不下课。我们只好对老师说："老师，该下课了。下课铃两分钟之前就响过了。"
10. 给何小英打电话之前我都看看几点钟，因为我怕她在上课。

二、用中文回答问题。
　　Answer the questions using Chinese.

1. 你刚刚接了一个电话吗？那个电话是谁打来的？
2. 你应该几点钟到老师的办公室来？
3. 你喜欢和谁一起打乒乓球？
4. 你每天自己做作业，还是和同学们一起做作业？
5. 谁的电话铃响？你听见了吗？
6. 听写的时候你们可以看书吗？
7. 你能记住每一门课的作业吗？如果记不住怎么办？
8. 你每次出门都带手机吗？如果忘了带电话怎么办？
9. 在哪门课上老师常常给你们讲故事？学生们喜欢听老师的故事吗？

10. 在汉语课上，你们常常用中文还是用英文回答老师的问题？

11. 你们学习词汇花时间多，还是学习语法花时间多？

12. 学生们可以在图书馆里打电话吗？可以在上课的时候接电话吗？

13. 你的手机是新的吗？这是你的第几个手机？谁给你买的这个手机？这个手机好用吗？

14. 你什么时候说"糟糕"？觉得蛋糕好吃的时候说，还是觉得考试没考好的时候说"糟糕"？

15. 在英语课上，你们每天都有作业吗？常常有什么作业？口头作业多还是笔头作业多？

第八课

笔试

第一部分　Part I

姓名 _____　　　得分 _____

一、发音。

Pronunciation: Circle the syllable that you hear. 10%

1. qī mò kǎo shì / qǐ mò kāo shī
2. zì wǒ jiè shào / zì wǒ jiē shǎo
3. tí yù huǒ dòng / tǐ yù huó dòng
4. shēng rì kuài lè / shèng rì kuái lè
5. tíng shuō dù xiě / tīng shuō dú xiě
6. jiē rán bù tōng / jié rán bù tóng
7. fǎ guó chú shī / fǎ guō chú shī
8. yǔ yīn liàn xí / yǔ yōn liàn xī
9. lián qú bǐ cài / lán qiú bǐ sài
10. xióng dí jiē mèi / xiōng dì jiě mèi

二、对不对?

Logical 对 or not logical 不对? Listen carefully and determine if the answer is logical with respect to the question. 12%

1. 对　　　不对
2. 对　　　不对
3. 对　　　不对
4. 对　　　不对
5. 对　　　不对
6. 对　　　不对

三、听力。

Choose "yes" or "no" after listening to the passage and comments. 9%

1. 对　　不对　　　2. 对　　不对　　　3. 对　　不对

61

四、请用完整的中文句子回答问题。
Answer the questions with complete sentences using Chinese. 20%

1.
2.
3.
4.
5.
6.
7.
8.
9.
10.

五、用下列词语造句。

Write a sentence with each of the following words and expressions. 15%

1. 作为

2. 因此

3. 或者

4. 当然

5. 不但……而且

六、请用中文写一篇短文 (至少一百二十个字)，谈谈你的理想.
Write a mini-composition (with at least 120 characters) using Chinese about your ideal profession for the future. 15%

我的理想

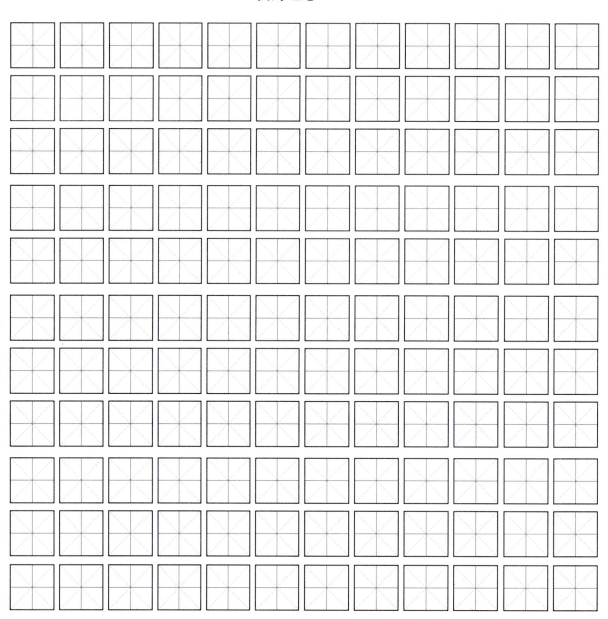

请把第一部分交给老师，然后开始第二部分。
Please turn in this first part before starting the second.

第二部分 Part II

姓名 _____

七、请用适当的量词填空。
Fill in the blanks with appropriate measure words. 10%

1. "三国演义"是一 _____ 中国小说。

2. 他有一 _____ 很高的理想？

3. 今天我们的作业是写一 _____ 五百字的作文。

4. 这 _____ 会计师做事很认真。

5. 马友友是一 _____ 出色的音乐家。

6. 在数学课上你们解了几 _____ 题。

7. 今天在中文课上我造了五 _____ 句子。

8. 那 _____ 画是谁画的？

9. 这是一 _____ 大家庭。

10. 老师给了我们三 _____ 作文题目。

八、文化点滴：请用英文回答下列问题。
Culture Notes: Answer the following questions using English: 9%

1. What are the two different writing systems in Chinese?
   _____

2. Who simplified some of the Chinese characters and for what reason?
   _____

3. Where are the two different writing systems used?
   _____

4. Identify these characters and the difference between them in terms of writing system:

_____

     語 语   们 們

5. What kind of writing system are you learning with *Elementary Chinese: Learning through Practice?*

_____

口语考试

一、朗读下列句子。
   Read aloud the following sentences.

   1. 我听说很多男学生想当工程师,很多女学生想当会计师。

   2. 我读了不少海明威的作品,最喜欢的还是"老人与海"。

   3. 爱迪生 (ài dí shēng Thomas Edison) 是美国人。他只上了三年小学,可是他发明了电和电话;他是一个科学家。

   4. 白文生成家立业的时候只有二十二岁,现在他应该有五十多岁了。

   5. 谢珍妮到底是哪一年结婚的,没有人能记得住了。

   6. 我们大家都是家庭和社会的成员。

   7. 我们认识这个邮递员。除了星期天以外,我们天天都能看见他。

   8. 我爸爸二十岁开始当飞行员,到现在有二十七年了。

   9. 我弟弟最大的理想是当工程师;他说没有人能改变他的想法。

   10. 作为警察,您给社会做了很多了不起的好事;作为家庭的一员,您是我们最好的爸爸。

二、用中文回答问题。
   Answer the questions using Chinese.

   1. 你是一个做事认真的学生吗?

   2. 你家里有人是厨师吗?

   3. 你的理想是什么?

   4. 当警察是谁的理想?

   5. 大家都在等你,你到底想不想和我们一起去长城公园?

   6. 在你的国家,你觉得谁是最出色的作家?

   7. 你读过赛珍珠的作品吗?你喜欢吗?

   8. 在朋友中,你最理解谁?谁最理解你?

9. 你喜欢分析问题吗？喜欢自己分析，还是和同学们一起分析？

10. 周伟石上了很多数学和物理课，你觉得他的理想是什么？

11. 在学校里，除了老师以外，还有做什么工作的人？

12. 如果当医生是你的理想，现在你应该做什么？

13. 白珍妮开始想当画家，她为什么改变了理想？

14. 你认为谁是一个了不起的人？为什么？

15. 在英文课上你们常常写作文吗？最长的作文要写多少个字？你最喜欢的作文题目是什么？